HOW TO BECOME A BETTER PARTNER

THE SECRET TO BECOME THE GREATEST PARTNER IN YOUR RELAYIONSHIP

By

Dr. Smith Matthew

Copyright@2022. Dr. Smith Matthew

All Right Reserved

TABLE OF CONTENTS

INTRODUCTION

Want more fun in your relationship?

Do you feel that things are not as good as they should be? Are you and your love partner having arguments that you think could be easily avoided? Answer yes to any of these questions. If so, this book is the answer to your prayers. This book will give you all the information you need to become a better partner or maintain a relationship. This book is everything you need to be a better lover, spouse or partner. This book will give you tips on how to be a better partner and have a lasting relationship and marriage.

This book is a guide on how to build true intimacy, find genuine love, and be truly happy in a relationship. Find the things you must do yourself, the things you and your partner must do together and many more things that will help you to have your dream relationship.

Read this book and apply the knowledge it contains into your relationship and you will see that your relationship can be all that you have longed-for. How to become a better partner:

Discover five tips to becoming a better partner in your relationship is a book that gives insight on the dos and don'ts in a relationship.

Relationships can become exhausting when handled the wrong way and it becomes frustrating when you find it difficult to understand your partner. Mastery of this simple skill will enable you to:

• Calm (and sometimes even eliminate) the concerns, fears, and uncertainties of others Increase feelings of love, respect, and appreciation in your romantic relationships

• Quickly resolve, or even prevent, arguments

• Help others become open to your point of view

• Provide support and encouragement to others, even when you don't know how to "fix" the problem

• Give advice and feedback that sticks

Do you want more out of your relationship? Feel like things just are not as good as they could be? Are you and your love partner having arguments that you think could be easily avoided, and would you like them to be? Above all, do you think your relationship is worth salvaging? If you answered yes to some, if not all, this book is the answer to your prayers. In this book you will find all the information you need to improve or save your relationship. This book is a guide on how to build true intimacy, find genuine love, and be truly happy in your relationship.

CHAPTER 1

WHAT YOU AND YOUR PARTNER NEED TO DO TOGETHER

Relationship myths, the golden rules of relationships, and much more to help you build the relationship of your dreams.

Please read this book and apply the knowledge it contains to your relationships.   Are you ready to   leave your partner but feel trapped financially and emotionally? Want to move but are afraid to move alone?

Get guidance from someone who has done it don't come too fast. Let the relationship develop at your own pace. If she plays too fast, it will almost certainly scare her, and as you continue to hang out with her, your feelings for her will gradually grow stronger.

Take courage, Most girls prefer someone who is ego-free
and confident.

A. Approach them and start a simple conversation. She
gets a hint that you're interested in her.

Start with a simple conversation starter:

• "That's a really nice dress. Where did it come from?"

• "Excuse me, I'm here. I just arrived; can you tell me
where the library is?"

• "Hello, my name is {Alex}. You look interesting to talk
to.

Staying with other girls and taking care of their daily lives.
This is not the same as flirting with other girls
and probably not a good move.

B. Tell girls that you're genuinely interested in what other girls think of you as a safe, trustworthy, and easy-going person when you're with them.

If other girls stand up indirectly like that, you've taken a big step.

• Be friends with her friends if it's not a big step. I know it can be overwhelming, but give it a try. If her friends like you, you are more likely to win her over. After all, a girl often asks her friends for advice or a second opinion. Make sure they appreciate you.

Practice good hygiene and personal hygiene. Women take pride in their clean smell and appearance. That said, if a man has good hygiene, it works very well for her. Conversely, poor hygiene is usually an immediate deal-breaker

C. Believe it or not, fresh, clean-smelling hair
is really a good thing—and a fresh-smelling body is
a must. Here are three things you can do
right away to improve your hygiene. If you can
afford it, it's better to be too clean than not clean
enough. Be proud of how clean you are and how
good you smell. This step is essential, especially if
you play sports

Shave and groom your facial hair daily. Most
women prefer men with no facial hair. It's
spiky and won't look good unless you're an
adult. Shave that stubble every day.

Use deodorant instead of cologne. Many men
believe that cologne can "mask" their natural
body odor. Instead, BO and
cologne mixed together stink so bad.

Girls would rather not smell you at all than smell

this cologne. If you must spray perfume, do so very lightly.

Make me laugh, make me happier. You can get a

lot more this way. But don't take advantage of it. Make her

your best friend first and then take it slow. A girl needs to

know that she can trust you and that you don't break her

heart because you really care about her.

Be honest and trustworthy. Compliments, flirting,

teasing, and attention - none of it matters unless

you really care prize.

• You can disagree with her as long as you don't threaten

her, respect her opinion, or give a valid reason to disagree.

Do you know? She may respect you more if you

speak your mind to her.

Prove that you love her very much. Show her that you're

not just in love with her or wanting her.

Ask her about herself and talk to her. Don't move just to kiss her.

Listen to her talk and look into her eyes.

Compliment me. It's hard to compliment a girl. Everyone wants to feel good, but finding the right compliment is really hard. Not only that, but a little compliment goes a long way. When you're ready to show that you like her more than just her friend, keep these guidelines in mind.

• See how she sees herself. If she considers herself an athlete, strengthen her competitiveness and her athleticism. If she thinks she is someone who thinks of herself, compliment her on how smart she is. No matter what she thinks of herself, compliment that aspect of her the most.

• Stick to safe Praise about her personality

don't Praise her on her feminine side or overly compliment her looks. Girls want to feel cute, but they also want to feel that you respect their smarts and individuality. If you want to Praise a girl on her looks, stick to the next part. Try:

• Smile

• Hair

• Eyes

• Lips

• Clothes

• Style

• Try compliments like these. These are rough sketches, so feel free to come up with your own that are appropriate for the occasion and the girl. May feel that way, but I like how your mind works."

• "I like your eye color similar." Your dress. Do any of

your parents have blue eyes too?

Remember the color of her eyes. Do this by looking

at her as often as possible when you talk to her. It's not a

bad idea to do this with every woman you meet.

Practice flirting with her. You may have started flirting

with her a little by complimenting and talking to her. Now

it's time to level up and really show her what your game

is all about.

• Visualize success and be confident in whatever you

do. You can't flirt if you don't trust your ability to persuade

her. So do whatever you want, score the winning

touchdown, or wait until you win the science fair and start

flirting.

CHAPTER 2

BREAK THROUGH THE TOUCH BARRIER

Start gently touching her in a safe, non-threatening area. Lightly touch her hand when pointing out or joking with the kicker. When you reassure her about something about her, immediately rub her back. If you want to get her attention, touch her shoulder.

• Teasing playfully. It is preferable that you tease her about her confidence or what she is good at so that she understands that you are teasing her, rather than insulting her. For example, if she's doing well in her school, "I don't want to take you on a science project because that means I'm always slack. Wasting her time please do not. It's a waste of time and takes the relationship down the wrong path. If you start a relationship with something wrong (such as being in a relationship for multiple years but not having a

girlfriend), you'll probably end up there. If you think the

girl is in a relationship for something and you are in a

relationship for another reason, don't just play around to

keep her. Tell her what you're looking for and make sure

she understands what's really important to her.

•Don't force yourself to play unless it works for

sure. Believe it or not, some people try to play hard to get

it. And most of the time, the girl fails

because she misinterprets her distance as cold.

Being consistently good. Most girls have someone they

can trust and turn to if something goes wrong.

Please let her know you are there. If you know she has

plans after work or school, ask how she's been doing.

She will eventually get her cue if you show that you

like her. She doesn't even have to come out and say it. If

you say you will do something, do it. When leading a conversation, be prepared to lead. Girls (and boys) hate it when people say they'll do something and they never do it. Don't be those guys

• Build your reputation. She shouldn't have the reputation of someone she might not want to date, i.e.:

• Treat other girls kindly and don't disturb them.

• Have good friends who are willing to stand up for you when you need them.

• To be universally loved, respected and respected. When she's cold, let her wear your jacket. Taking it off her back and putting it on her makes it even more impressive, but make sure it's clean and smells right, this is a way to show a girl that you care about her she will feel safe and cared for be capable of what she is. Ask her about her day. It's an easy way to show her that you're interested in what she's doing and that you care about her. Once she starts talking,

she needs to give her full attention. Look

in her eyes MOST importantly, don't interrupt. Ask her her

questions to show her that you are listening and share

her opinion if you have any. Share her feelings with her.

When she gets her perfect score on her math

test, congratulate her! If she feels bad, let her know that

you feel her pain and that you want to make her feel

better. Please ask her if there's anything you can do

to make her feel better.

• If you know a surefire way to cheer her up, use it when

she's feeling down. Maybe she likes a special kind

of froyo that's only two towns down south.

CHAPTER 3

LOVE HER WEIRDNESS

We all have things we don't like about people we like, but when this list includes too many big things, it becomes a problem. You have to love them for what makes them special, their uniqueness. Tell her.

• For example, if she is unsure about something, you have a great opportunity to make her feel better.

For example, "I love your freckles.

Simple things like this can lift her mood and show that you like her for all the right reasons, including her personality and looks. As we get to know them, we will probably be able to understand and understand this anxiety better. Instead of drawing attention to it, encourage them to forgive and look at all the other qualities that make them   great.

Make her feel like the prettiest girl in the world. You can say it directly. She girls love to be complimented and she wants to know she's beautiful, but especially in her new friendships, she shouldn't overdo it. Make her happy by telling   her   things   like "You   look great today" As   long   as you   are   honest and   mean business. Otherwise, they won't trust your opinion on other things. Develop good communication   skills.   Share   interesting things you think and stories about people you've met.

You've probably asked her a lot of questions, but she may not know you very well. Share the parts of yourself that you enjoy sharing, and perhaps even the parts of yourself that you are still afraid of. Don't be afraid to show her a   small   part of   yourself   that is   easy.

• Put yourself in their shoes.

What does she like to talk about and how does she react to her criticism?

What's different from other girls?

What is she proud of?

 Answer these questions from her perspective and plan her accordingly. If you haven't heard of her yet, ask her. Getting to the date phase is the hardest part. If you've been on a few dates, you'll know in no time if she's still the one of your dreams. But getting there can be difficult. Luckily, you are confident, calm, and planning. Things can get awkward when you call it dating. Instead, say something like, "Hey, I got her two tickets to this new movie on Saturday, but my boyfriend stopped."

Do you want to go?"

• Doing things that are exciting and get your heart rate up

will increase your chances of a successful date:

Haunted houses, theme parks with   roller   coasters,

horror movies. Dating,

• Be a gentleman, open the door for her, be on time

and pay for her date. Don't expect a kiss on the first

date. Please   make   yourself   comfortable.

Make her comfortable with every step and she should melt

into your arms. Always let her know you love her.

Love her for who she is, inside and out and show it. This is

the most important step. She will be more interested in a

relationship if she knows you love her.

CHAPTER 4

THE CENTRE OF INTEREST ON YOUR PARTNER
If you want to make a lasting change in your relationship, stop focusing on what your partner is and isn't doing and ask yourself: How can I be a better partner?" By asking how to be a better partner to your loved ones, you move to a world-minded level and put your partner's needs first. This does not mean denying yourself your needs. Let your partner know that you are there for them, that they can trust you, and that they can feel safe and secure in their vulnerability. Bonds of intimacy and connection are strengthened, and ultimately, you'll be able to do more than just be a good partner when your relationship becomes something special. Convey the positive feelings It takes time to make connections Small talk and communication are not the same thing. Many

relationships fall into the same routine with questions

like "How was your day?" and "What do you want to

do tonight?" We spend time together in front of the TV

instead of actually hooking up. But you can never know

what your partner needs without spending time

developing the relationship. Practical Relationship Skills

Communication is more than just speaking.

By listening intently, your partner not only feels heard, but

understood. Make eye

contact, provide nonverbal feedback, and focus on

what they're saying. Be open and accepting. Instead

of being your partner's harshest critic, be understanding.

Listen to your partner's point of view without judging

it. You relate to your partner and build trust

in that relationship. It addresses practical relationship

kills such as conflict resolution, being with your

partner, caring about what makes your partner

happy, and catching non-verbal cues.

Express gratefulness

Gratitude is essential in all areas of life,

including relationships. Instead of thinking of all the

things you like about your partner, tell them. Say "thank

you" and tell them exactly what you are grateful for. And

always share positive emotions. Feeling and expressing joy

and joy in the relationship will be your partner's weakness.

Provide safeguard whether someone is having a bad day or

a long-term problem, stress can negatively affect both

partners in a relationship. Remember that having your back

is part of learning how to be a great partner in

a relationship. Promise your unconditional support

when your partner is down. Being comfortable with your

partner is the first step to true intimacy. If you can be

vulnerable, you can learn how to be a good partner in a

relationship. An emotionally healthy relationship allows

you to share your thoughts, feelings, wants and needs

without fear of judgment or criticism. In return,

you don't judge your partner - you accept them for

who they are. Equal and fulfilling partnerships are not

possible. Actively share tasks such

as household chores and finances. Need incentives?

A study found that couples who shared household

chores more evenly maintained more intimacy than

those who had unequal arrangements

CHAPTER 5

BEST RELATIONSHIP ADVICES

1. Don't date your ex, he became your ex for a reason.

Your ex is part of your past, move on.

2. Almost 70% of family members date you don't

want to marry someone if you don't like them.

Marriages are very likely not to last and you are

unlikely to enjoy your relationship.

3. There is a distinct difference between dating for

love and dating for sex. Always understand

the primary reason you are in a relationship.

4 Never fall in love when you are lonely. The results

will be grim.

5. Never reveal your potential or secrets to the person

you are dating while you are dating.

6. Prioritize self-development over relationships,

the person you are in a relationship with can

leave you, but you cannot leave yourself.

7. Avoid relationships that seem too good at first.

Don't get carried away with love or sex if your partner

is in a hurry. Take it slow and be careful

because that's how people become

dependent on a narcissistic partner.

8. Give orders and don't date people who don't respect

you. The potential for emotional abuse is very high.

9. Don't date someone who doesn't know how to

give and only how to receive.

10. Don't date someone whose attitude is to

change their personality, attitude, or behavior.

Remember you can never raise an adult!

Never date an unattractive person. If in doubt, say NO.

Never date someone you just broke up with. He/she

may be rebounding. In fact, most of the time, yes.

Don't date someone who isn't as emotionally strong

as you are.

Don't rush. Rushing things will only lead to more

complications. Start slow. discover each other.

If your partner lies to you about small things,

he/she can lie to you about bigger things as

well. Please leave her immediately.

Lack of communication destroys relationships. Always

communicate with your partner about your problems

you can't cure someone you don't want to cure.

Savior Complex No more bullshit. You can pick up

the pieces and solve all your problems, but

you can't change someone who doesn't have

the will to change. People are who they are and will

remain so until they choose not to be. The hard truth is

that you can't "tame" a person. You are not responsible

for anyone. Communication is everything.

Talk about things. For better or worse. Be honest with

each other. Without communication, there is no

relationship. People who truly love you don't just hear

the answer, they understand it.

Don't give up when you're in trouble.

Most people are skeptical when faced with the

first problems in a relationship. But don't cut it here.

Relationships don't have to be perfect. It's pull and

push. Effort is required. There may be disagreements

and quarrels, but in the end there is still love. That is

the most important.

One way street

Efforts must be mutual. You shouldn't feel the need to

ask for respect or gratitude. This is the bare minimum.

Marry your best friend.

You should be 100% comfortable with your partner and her. You should feel safe and secure so that you can say anything and everything in front of them without being judged. Marry someone who makes you laugh until your stomach hurts and who enjoys each other's company after all these years. Marry your best friend